Rollin'

Motocross Cycles

by Jeff Savage

C A P S T O N E   P R E S S
M A N K A T O

Capstone Books are published by Capstone Press
151 Good Counsel Drive, P.O. Box 669, Mankato, Minnesota 56002
http://www.capstone-press.com

Library of Congress Cataloging-in-Publication Data
Savage, Jeff, 1961-
  Motocross cycles / Jeff Savage.
  p. cm.
  Includes bibliographical references and index.
  Summary: Provides an overview of motocross racing, describing the
history of the sport, the features of the motorcycles, and the racing
competitions.
  ISBN 1-56065-370-1
  1. Motorcycles, Racing--Juvenile literature. [1. Motorcycle racing.
2. Motocross.] I. Title.
TL440.15.S29 1996
796.7'56--dc20

                                                    95-47672
                                                      CIP
                                                       AC

Photo credit
All photos by Peter Ford

Table of Contents

Words in **boldface** type in the text are defined
in the Glossary in the back of this book.

Chapter 1

International Sport

Motocross races are motorcycle races on dirt tracks. The words "motorcycle" and "cross country" were combined to form the word "motocross."

Motocross is one of the most physically demanding sports in the world. Riders have to be in top shape to drive their bikes over rough ground.

Motocross is an international sport. Thousands of professional and amateur riders compete around the world. Often more than 100 motocross events take place in the United States and Canada during a weekend.

Motocross is a year-round sport. All races are held outdoors. Similar races held indoors are called supercross.

Motocross races are held on dirt tracks.

Chapter 2
History

The motorcycle was invented in 1885. The first motorcycle was a bicycle with a gasoline engine attached under the seat. The words "motor" and "bicycle" were combined to form the word "motorcycle."

The first motorcycles were large machines that moved slowly. They were designed to be driven only on paved roads.

By 1910, motorcycle riders demanded larger gas tanks, softer seats, and better shock absorbers. American companies such as Harley-Davidson, Mitchell, Indian, and Royal

Motocross is a year-round, international sport.

competed to make a more comfortable motorcycle.

Racing

Motorcycle companies knew the public loved speed. They made motorcycles that could go as fast as 60 miles (96 kilometers) per hour. Soon, motorcycle races were being held everywhere. Faster motorcycles were built especially for racing.

In 1924, a race was held in England. It was called a motorcycle scramble. It was similar to the motocross racing of today. But the public did not show much interest in the race.

The First Motocross

In 1947, Roland Poirer organized the first motocross race in Paris, France. It was staged on rough ground. Hills, jumps, and hairpin turns were part of the course.

The race was called Motocross des Nations. That means motocross of the nations in French.

Hairpin turns are important parts of motocross courses.

Riders from many countries competed in the race. It was a success. It is still held in France every year.

North America Discovers Racing

Troops coming home after World War II (1939-1945) brought motocross to North America. Soon, European companies began selling motocross cycles in the United States

Motocross is one of the most physically demanding sports in the world.

It is common for more than 100 motocross events to take place in the United States and Canada on any weekend.

and Canada. Two English companies, Norton and BSA, and a Belgian company, FN, made large cycles that were used in most races.

The Bikes Improve

Ten years later, Husqvarna, a Swedish company, introduced a lighter motorcycle that was easier to control. Other European companies such as Norton, BMW, and Triumph followed Husqvarna's lead.

In the 1960s, motocross racers everywhere wanted cycles that were easier to handle. Japanese companies responded by making machines with smaller engines.

Bombardier, a company in Quebec, Canada, produced the popular Can Am motocross bike in the 1970s. Today, Honda, Suzuki, Yamaha, and Kawasaki make high-speed, lightweight bikes. They are used by professionals and amateurs in all classes.

Today, the most popular bikes are made by Honda, Suzuki, Yamaha, and Kawasaki.

Motocross Expansion

In 1967, Edison Dye, a promoter, brought a group of skilled European riders to California for a race. The Europeans were matched against a group of amateur North American riders. The Europeans won easily.

But Dye's plan worked. Motocross became a hit on the West Coast. The sport's popularity spread quickly. Soon, young riders throughout North America were dreaming of becoming the next great motocross racer.

Motocross events are held in cities from coast to coast.

Chapter 3
Parts and Safety Gear

Motocross cycles come in several sizes. Size is measured in cubic centimeters (cc's). The more cc's an engine has, the bigger and more powerful it is.

The smallest cycle is the 50cc minibike. It is used by children as young as five years old. The three sizes used in professional races are 125cc, 250cc, and 500cc.

The Engine

Motocross cycles are powered by gasoline-fueled **internal combustion** engines. The

Motocross engines are made of lightweight aluminum.

engines are made mostly of lightweight aluminum.

In an internal combustion engine, a mixture of fuel and air is sprayed into a **cylinder**. The cylinder is shaped like a hollow tube. Inside the cylinder is a plug called a **piston**.

The fuel inside the cylinder is ignited by a **spark plug**. Heated air from the burning fuel pushes down on the piston.

The piston is connected to a **crankshaft**. When the piston moves, the crankshaft triggers the **power train**.

The size of the cylinder, measured in cubic centimeters, is the size of the engine. For example, there are 250 cubic centimeters inside the cylinder of a 250cc motocross bike.

Ports

Ports are small holes inside the cylinder. Gasoline flows through intake ports. Air flows through exhaust ports.

The size of the cylinder, measured in cubic centimeters, is the size of the engine.

Ports are widened on motocross bikes. This allows more fuel and air to pass through. Wider ports give the engine more top-end power. Bikes with more top-end power perform well on the wide-open motocross courses.

Ports are narrowed for supercross bikes which are raced on indoor tracks. Narrow ports give the engine more bottom-end power. Bikes with more bottom-end power perform better on the tight, sharp supercross tracks.

Exhaust Systems

The exhaust system on motocross bikes is modified to increase power. The exhaust pipes are widened to produce more top-end power.

The exhaust system on most bikes is made of aluminum or an **alloy**. The system on the best bikes is usually made of titanium, an especially durable metal.

The Power Train

The power train controls the amount of power sent from the engine to the rear wheel.

The ports in motocross engines are widened to give the cycles more top-end power.

There are three parts to the power train. They are the **clutch**, the **gearbox**, and the **drive chain**.

The clutch connects the power train to the engine. The driver controls the clutch by squeezing a lever with his or her left hand. When the clutch is engaged, the engine is not connected to the gearbox and drive chain.

The clutch must be disengaged to shift gears. Motocross bikes usually have five gears. The gears are housed in a gearbox.

The driver changes gears by tapping or lifting a lever with his or her left foot. A popular shifting pattern is called one down, four up. The driver taps the lever down once for first gear. He or she lifts the lever up for second, third, fourth, and fifth gears.

When the clutch is engaged, the drive chain transfers the engine's power to the rear wheel. When a gear is changed, the drive chain speeds up or slows down the rear wheel.

A motocross bike's knobby tires provide excellent traction in mud and loose dirt.

Tires

Standard street motorcycles have tires with smooth tread. Motocross bikes use heavy-duty tires to get better traction on rough ground.

Motocross tires, called knobby tires, have square, spoked treads. They provide excellent traction in mud and loose dirt.

The front tire is about two inches (five centimeters) bigger in diameter than the rear tire. The front tire is also narrower than the rear tire. The bigger, narrower tire offers better turning control.

Rims, Forks, and Shocks

Motocross tires are supported by rims made of reinforced aluminum. They are lighter and stronger than standard motorcycle rims.

The front wheel of a motorcycle is connected to the handlebars by the front fork. Motocross forks are made of aluminum. They take a pounding. Two heavy-duty shock absorbers are built into the front fork. The

The drive chain transfers power from the engine to the rear wheel.

The exhaust pipes on motocross bikes are widened to give the cycles more power.

shock absorbers provide a cushion during hard landings.

In the late 1980s, top drivers experimented with their front forks. They turned the forks upside down. The inverted forks allowed more clearance under the bike. Drivers could more easily avoid rocks and debris with the extra clearance.

In the mid-1990s, technicians designed new forks that met drivers' demands for clearance. These new forks are more durable than the inverted forks. Most racers have returned to right-side-up forks. These forks are made of titanium.

Frames and Brakes

Motocross frames are especially durable. The frames are raised so the bikes can pass over rocks and debris.

Riders sometimes ignore the brakes for long spells. But when they need them, the brakes are critical. Sometimes, brakes are all that keep a rider from straying off the course.

The driver works the rear brake by pressing a lever with the right foot. The front brake is

controlled by squeezing a lever with the right hand.

Safety Gear

Motocross racing is a dangerous sport. Professional racers do not plan to crash, but they prepare for the worst. Riders wear a complete set of protective gear. A full set includes a helmet, gloves, boots, and body armor.

The proper helmet is made either of **Kevlar** or a hard plastic. All helmets have face protectors.

Motocross gloves are made of leather or hard plastic. Motocross riders wear leather boots. The boots have metal toecaps because riders often scrape the ground with their feet.

Racers wear body armor pieces made of hard plastic. The body armor is worn inside the jersey and pants. Body armor covers the chest, shoulders, thighs, knees, and elbows.

A full set of protective gear includes a helmet, gloves, boots, and body armor.

Chapter 4

Stock Bikes and Factory Bikes

Motocross bikes sold at dealerships are called **stock bikes**. Motocross bikes used by professional racers are called **factory bikes**. Factory bikes are more powerful than stock bikes.

The Works

A factory bike is sometimes called a **works bike**. Works bikes contain all the upgrades available, or the works.

Top riders add personal touches to works bikes. Some raise or lower the handlebars a few centimeters. Some change the grips

The motocross bikes used by professional racers are called factory bikes.

because they prefer a different material. Some adjust the seat or lower the foot pegs.

New Bikes

Motorcycle makers follow a specific procedure when creating new motorcycles. They produce protos, pre-pros, and one-offs. They test them on private tracks.

Proto is short for prototype. A proto is a bike with features that are little more than ideas. The company may eventually include a few of the new features on its finished model, or it may cancel them all. It depends on how the tests go.

A pre-pro is a pre-production version of the finished model. About 100 pre-pros are made to be tested on private tracks by company drivers.

One-offs are sold to the public so companies can measure people's interest. Then the company makes a few final adjustments. Finally, the production line rolls out the new motorcycle.

A factory bike is sometimes called a works bike. Works bikes have all the upgrades available, or the works.

Chapter 5

The Races

Motocross races take place on tracks that vary in length from one to three miles (two to five kilometers). The tracks have many natural and man-made hazards.

Usually, the track surface is watered down and plowed before a race. The rough surface provides better traction for the motorcycles.

The starting area is wide enough to fit as many as 30 racers lined up side-by-side. The track narrows to just a few feet in spots. The changing width adds more challenge to the course.

Whoop-de-dos are rows of bumps that riders try to skip over. Riders may take the bumps one at a time or clear them completely

Motocross tracks have both natural and man-made hazards.

in one long jump. **Berms** are fast turns banked to the inside. Gullies, hills, water holes, mud holes, and sharp corners are among the other obstacles racers must overcome.

Motos

Motocross races have two **heats**. A heat is called a moto. Each moto is the same distance, usually from 15 to 25 laps around the track. A moto lasts about 45 minutes.

In the motos, riders earn points based on their finishing positions. The winner gets one point for a first-place finish. Second place gets two points. Third place gets three points, and so on.

The winner of the overall event is the rider with the lowest point total after both motos. A rider might finish second twice and earn four total points. Another rider might win the first moto, but finish fifth in the second moto. That rider earns six total points. The first rider finishes ahead in the overall standings.

The bike a rider brings to the starting line for the first moto is the qualified cycle. A rider

Riders earn points based on their finishing positions.

cannot change bikes. The qualified cycle is the one cycle a rider can use during a day's motos.

Events and Circuits

Major motocross races are called events. They are held around the world. Events are divided into classes according to engine size.

A circuit is a series of events sanctioned by an organization. To sanction an event is to organize it, promote it, and govern it. Sanctioning organizations make the rules for an event.

The World Championship Motocross Series is a 15-event circuit that runs each year from March to August. Most of the events are held in Europe.

The American Motorcyclist Association (AMA) sanctions motocross events. It sanctions 16 indoor events and 12 outdoor events each year in the United States. The AMA also sanctions hundreds of amateur motocrosses each year.

Motocross tracks are usually watered down and plowed before a race to give the cycles better traction.

Berms are fast turns banked to the inside.

The Canadian Motorcycle Association (CMA) sanctions four national professional events each year. The CMA also sponsors hundreds of local events.

All for the Thrill

The world of motocross racing is an exciting one. Riders and spectators agree that motocross racing is a thrilling sport.

The riders jockey for position. Some cycles crash. From the starting line to the finish line, the action is nonstop.

That is excitement. That is motocross.

Glossary

alloy—two or more metals mixed together
berm—turn banked to the inside
clutch—lever that allows the driver to shift gears
crankshaft—rod connected to the pistons
cylinder—can-shaped area of an engine that holds the pistons where gas is ignited
drive chain—large chain connecting the gears to the rear wheels
factory bikes—powerful motocross bikes used in competition
gearbox—box that houses gears
heat—preliminary round of a race
Kevlar—a strong fiber
internal combustion—process in which gasoline burns and expands inside the cylinder
piston—plug inside the cylinder that connects to the crankshaft
power train—system that controls the power sent to the rear wheel

spark plug—thumb-sized part in the engine that receives an electric charge and ignites the gasoline in the cylinder

stock bikes—motocross bikes sold at dealerships

whoop-de-dos—a series of bumps on a track

works bike—a factory bike that has the latest features

To Learn More

Carser, S.X. *Motocross Cycles.* Mankato, Minn.: Capstone Press, 1992.

Estrem, Paul. *Motocross Cycles.* New York: Crestwood House, 1987.

Jeffries, David. *Trail Bikes and Motocross.* New York: Warwick Press, 1990.

Young, Jesse. *Motocross Racing.* Minneapolis: Capstone Press, 1995.

You can read articles about motocross in *Dirt Rider* and *Motocross Action* magazines.

Useful Addresses

American Motorcyclists Association
33 College View Road
Westerville, OH 43081-1484

Canadian Motorcycle Association
P.O. Box 448
Hamilton, ON L8L 8C4
Canada

Cycle News
2201 Cherry Avenue
Long Beach, CA 90806

SRO Motorsports
477 East Butterfield Road
Lombard, IL 60148

Index